wOrk-wiSe

Your guide to work-related learning and enterprise education

Chris Vidler

www.heinemann.co.uk
✓ Free online support
✓ Useful weblinks
✓ 24 hour online ordering

01865 888058

Heinemann Educational Publishers
Halley Court, Jordan Hill, Oxford OX2 8EJ
Part of Harcourt Education

Heinemann is the registered trademark of
Harcourt Education Limited

© Harcourt Education, 2005

First published 2005

10 09 08 07 06 05

10 9 8 7 6 5 4 3 2 1

British Library Cataloguing in Publication Data is available
from the British Library on request.

10-digit ISBN: 0 435 32483 7
13-digit ISBN: 978 0 435 32283 4

To Grace and Fleur, who inspired much of this handbook.

Copyright notice

All rights reserved. No part of this publication may be reproduced in any form or by any means (including photocopying or storing it in any medium by electronic means and whether or not transiently or incidentally to some other use of this publication) without the written permission of the copyright owner, except in accordance with the provisions of the Copyright, Designs and Patents Act 1988 or under the terms of a licence issued by the Copyright Licensing Agency, 90 Tottenham Court Road, London W1T 4LP. Applications for the copyright owner's written permission should be addressed to the publisher.

Produced by Kamae Design

Original illustrations © Harcourt Education Limited, 2005

Printed by Thomsons Litho Ltd

Picture research by Christine Martin

Acknowledgements
Every effort has been made to contact copyright holders of material reproduced in this book. Any omissions will be rectified in subsequent printings if notice is given to the publishers.

Photographs
Alamy Images p.58; Empics pp.31, 43; Equal Opportunities Commission p.57; Eyewire p.23; Fairtrade Foundation p.13 (both); Getty Images/PhotoDisc p.17; Harcourt Education Ltd/Peter Evans p.18; Harcourt Education Ltd/Gareth Boden pp.62, 86(top); Mary Evans Photo Library p.62 (bottom); Rex Features pp.47, 84; Totaljobs.com p.71; the photo on p.27 is reproduced courtesy of Apple.

Written sources
The article on page 57 is reproduced by kind permission of the Press Association.

The views in this work are solely those of the author and not necessarily those of Ofsted or Oxfam. Oxfam Activities Limited is a wholly owned subsdiary of Oxfam, registered charity number 202918 and donates all of its profits to Oxfam.

Contents

Introduction	4
Getting started	
1 Skills for life	10
2 Benchmarking	14
3 Who are you?	16
4 Knowing where you are going	18
How do businesses work?	
5 What's the big deal about work?	20
6 Different working environments	22
7 Business objectives	24
8 Business organizations	26
9 Risks and rewards	30
10 Size matters	32
11 Motivation – why even think about working?	34
Work experience	
12 Work experience – long-term planning	36
13 Getting the most out of work experience	38
Making things happen	
14 Problem-solving	42
15 Doing it for yourself	46
16 Business for real	50
More about work	
17 Rules in the workplace	54
18 Workers' rights	56
19 Conflict in the workplace	58
20 Health and safety	60
21 Work can be everywhere!	62
22 Meeting real people	66
23 Same but different	68
Your choice	
24 Should I stay or should I go?	70
25 Moving on	72
26 Getting ready for the careers interview	74
27 Applying for a job	78
28 Interview technique	84
29 Perils of plastic	88
Conclusion	91
Glossary	93
Index	95

Introduction

Welcome to *Work-Wise*! The government has decided to improve the way that schools prepare students for the world of work, and your school will have designed a special programme to meet this requirement. This probably includes:

- work experience
- enterprise education
- careers preparation
- learning about different types of business
- having links with local businesses.

Different schools organize this aspect of your learning in different ways. Many include it in personal, social and health education (PSHE), others in tutor time and some dedicate whole days to learning about work.

This book has been designed and written to enable you to keep track of learning about work, and it is specifically designed to help you sort out what you might do when you have finished school. When you finish Year 11 we want you to be as well informed as possible about future careers and jobs. This does not mean to say that you have to have everything sorted, but it is important that you have a good understanding of the consequences of choices that you might make during Years 10 and 11. There are no right and wrong answers about sorting out your life, but at least you can be better informed.

This book should help you to develop a clearer understanding of:

- the kind of person you are, including the skills you have and those that are required in different jobs
- what businesses and the world of work are really like
- what you might have to do to be successful in work

- some of the challenges and problems you might face
- managing your finances.

This structure is reflected in this book. However, we hope that as you progress through the book you will learn more about yourself and therefore will return to review the progress you are making in deciding about a possible career.

Something to think about when learning about work is that none of us are the same, and we find out about work in lots of different ways. Schools help this process by arranging work experience, mock interviews and visits outside school, but a lot of finding out about work is something that you do outside of school. This book is designed to help you and other students bring together all these experiences and to help prepare you for the world of work. You might want to keep this handbook with you so you can record what you find out about work and yourself in different lessons and during different activities.

Work-Wise is designed to be used as flexibly as possible. As noted earlier, schools organize work-related and enterprise education differently. If you have chosen to do business studies, applied or vocational subjects, you will find considerable overlap between *Work-Wise* and your normal classes. For the rest of you, learning about work could crop up in any of the subjects you take. We also learn about work in different ways – there are all the things that you already know from home, your friends and what you see on television and in films. You might also have a part-time job, which means you are already in the workplace. Doing everyday things, such as shopping, teaches you about how the world of business works and possible careers.

This book is a place where you bring all these different threads together so that by the end of Year 11 you have a record, almost a diary, which you can refer to when it comes to making big decisions. It can help you move on into the world of work or further education.

Over to you

All students in Years 10 and 11 have to do work-related learning and enterprise education. Some schools use 'off timetable days' while others include this across the curriculum. Find out when and where you will be doing work-related learning and enterprise education, and complete the timetable and time lines below – these will help prompt you when you are going to use this book. Fill in the timetable to show the lessons in which you are learning about work and enterprise.

Work-related learning timetable

Week 1

	1	2	3	4	5	6	7
Monday							
Tuesday							
Wednesday							
Thursday							
Friday							

Week 2

	1	2	3	4	5	6	7
Monday							
Tuesday							
Wednesday							
Thursday							
Friday							

Work-related learning time line

During Years 10 and 11 you will be doing things linked to work-related learning and enterprise at different times. For example, the time for work experience in your school is probably set. Fill in the time line below when you know what is happening through the year. You should also decide on times to review your progress in skills development – at least once every term (see pages 16–17 for more information on this).

Date	Work-related activity
Term 1	
Term 2	
Term 3	
Term 4	

Helicopter vision

The diagram below shows how the different elements of *Work-Wise* link together, and how they connect to work-related learning and enterprise education.

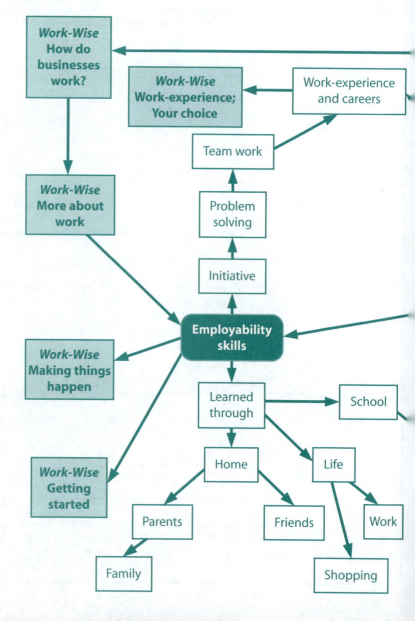

Mind maps, spider diagrams or 'brain dumps' are useful tools for getting an overview of a subject or a problem. Some people find this kind of activity particularly helpful in sorting out complex issues and to remember key elements. They can be used in any subject area or context. As you're working through *Work-Wise* you might want to use this type of activity to help you think through problems. Start by writing the problem in the centre and then use arrows and colours to write down your ideas.

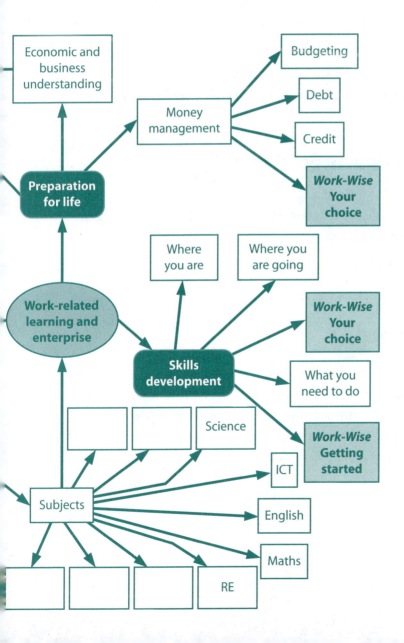

1 Skills for life

There is a range of skills that you need to develop to be successful in later life. They overlap with, but do not necessarily correspond to, the subjects you take or the way skills are described in your school. However, ask most students, teachers or employers what they think you need to get on in life and you will end up with a list of skills like the one below.

Look at the list and underneath each skill identify the subjects you take that help you to develop each of these skills. Try to give at least one example of each.

Communication

We have to be able to communicate clearly with each other. This includes speaking, writing and reading skills. You learn communication skills in all your subjects and especially in English.

Learned in _____

_____

ICT

It is hard to think of a job that does not involve some use of ICT – using the Internet for research, writing letters or compiling spreadsheets, for example. Most of us use computers at home to make life easier. You may take a separate ICT course and you probably develop IT skills in some of your other subjects.

Learned in _____

_____

Numeracy

Not maths, but numeracy. This means being able to work out your money, make a budget and keep to it. It also covers understanding costs, income, mortgages and tax. You may cover this in your maths classes. For some, it will be part of PSHE or social education.

Learned in _____

_____

Team work

In both your working and social lives most people would agree that you have to get on with other people. You need to learn how to work with others, which means knowing your own strengths and weaknesses, being prepared to take responsibility, finding ways of avoiding conflict and sometimes being a leader. Many employers put team-working skills at the top of their list.

Learned in _____

_____

Problem-solving

Life and work can be seen as an enormous problem-solving exercise. How do you juggle the demands of your social life with the demands of your teachers and parents? Is there a better way of dealing with something? What is the best way of getting from A to B? Is there a cheaper option? How do you learn these skills in school?

Learned in _____

_____

Managing yourself

This means sorting out your priorities and your time, getting organized and taking charge of your own learning. Does your school help you to manage and organize yourself?

Learned in _____

_____

Employability

Sooner or later, the chances are that you will want to make someone want to employ you. Qualifications count for something but reliability, perseverance or 'stickability', personal hygiene and being able to work without direct supervision are also important factors that employers look for.

Learned in _____

_____

Understanding about businesses

Sorting out what you might do in life requires knowing about the real world of businesses and how they work. You will probably all do work experience and have some kind of careers advice. You might also take business studies.

Learned in _____

_____

Creativity

This is not just for the gifted artist or sports person. All of us can be creative in different ways. For example, you might come up with a creative way of solving a problem. All of us will need to be creative in trying to make a success of our lives. How do you learn to be creative?

Learned in _____

_____

Morals and ethics

Is it ok to cheat, lie and rip other people off? Discriminate and exploit? Do the ends justify the means? We must have a sense of right and wrong in the world of work and enterprise as in the rest of our lives.

Some products and methods of production are more ethical than others. The Fairtrade Mark ensures that Third World Producers are paid a fair price for their products that will at least cover the costs of production.

Learned in _____

_____

This book is intended to help you keep track of how you develop these skills, especially those that might appear new or different. Each skill has been given an icon. These will be used throughout the book to remind you which skills are being discussed. You will also be required to assess your own progress in developing these skills for life. You might want to set aside time in the chart on page 7 to review your skill development.

2 Benchmarking

Work-Wise is designed to put you more in charge of your learning. In Section 1 we identified the ten skills needed for employment and enterprise. In this section you need to sort out your starting point. Companies and other organizations call this process **benchmarking** to measure their progress and success. This involves agreeing a starting point and assessing progress at agreed intervals. This might be something simple like recording the number of customer complaints received in a given period, setting goals such as to improve customer service, and measuring the outcomes in the future.

Over to you

1. Take the ten skills outlined on pages 10–13 and assess your current level of competence and confidence. Use a 10-point scale, with 0 = absolutely no knowledge and 10 = total understanding and confidence. Put a pencil cross in the most appropriate box.

	0	1	2	3	4	5	6	7	8	9	10
Communication											
ICT											
Numeracy											
Team work											
Problem-solving											
Managing yourself											
Employability											
Understanding about businesses											
Creativity											
Morals and ethics											

(2) Compare and discuss your self-assessment with a friend and revise your scores if need be. When you are happy with your self-assessment, use a pen to confirm your judgements. Every individual has strengths in different areas, so your scores should not be the same for each skill.

(3) Choose three of the above skills that you would like to improve most. Record them in the chart below and say how you plan to improve. Repeat this process every time you review your skills development.

Skill	Where (Subject? In school? Out of school?)	How?

Moving on

This book is designed to help you improve your scores, especially for the most important of the lot – your self-confidence. Your teachers will be giving you opportunities to develop and practise these skills, but you need to keep a record of your progress. Record the scores you have given yourself and the date in the first row of the chart below. Return and complete further rows as your skills develop over the next two years.

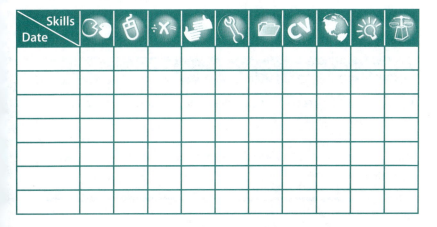

3 Who are you?

Do you see yourself as a child or an adult? The answer is probably somewhere between the two. You do not need to be reminded that being fourteen or fifteen can be confusing. Different people treat you in different ways. This can even apply to teachers! The main objective of this section of *Work-Wise* is to help you 'find out' what sort of person you are in relation to the world of work.

Think of yourself as being made up of thousands of different characteristics or **attributes**. Some of these are well formed and everyone would recognize them. Others are in development and, as this process of understanding ourselves lasts a lifetime, there are things about ourselves that we have yet to learn. This is all the 'you' side of things.

When it comes to the world of work there are thousands of different types of jobs and even more different potential employers. They want to employ workers who have a particular set of characteristics. This might all be written down in **job descriptions** or **person specifications**, but a lot will be hidden and unsaid. As you go through this book, you will have a better idea about the expectations of employers. We aim to help you recognize and develop those attributes that are likely to be most helpful when it comes to work.

This part of the book is designed to start you thinking about what you are like and also to give you some idea about the different expectations of employers.

Over to you

1. On a blank sheet of paper, write down the three things that you are good at.

2. Compare what you have done with a friend. Do they see you differently? Who is right?

Research

Find an adult, not a relation or a teacher, who knows you. Give them a pen and a piece of paper and ask them to choose three things that you are good at. Do not be embarrassed, and try to talk about what the adult has written down. You could do this with a recorder of some sort.

Over to you

I want people who are multi-skilled. I run a **'lean' business**, with everyone having to take responsibility. I want to recruit people who can take this on, work on their own and with their colleagues when appropriate.

What does this quote tell you about what skills employers might be looking for?

Research

Use the table below to list up to five attributes you would like to develop that may make you more employable. Think of ways in which you can develop these attributes and record these in the right column. Do not worry if you cannot come up with much at this stage – you can always return to this key question as you learn more about the world of work.

Attributes I can develop	Development strategies

4 Knowing where you are going

Most of us have doubts about our lives and what we do, even later on in life. This is not a reason for not planning for the future. It is time to think about possible careers.

Over to you

1) Survey your class about their thoughts on their intended careers. Use the following three categories.

   a) Haven't a clue.
   b) Definite idea.
   c) Some idea.

2) Produce a pie chart indicating the proportions of your class falling into these three categories.

Key
☐ Haven't a clue
☐ Definite idea
☐ Some idea

Your class may be unusual, but for most the biggest element will be the 'Some idea' segment.

3) Which category applies to you? Write this into the box below and give your main reasons.

Thinking about what you want to do when you finish your education can be difficult and even frightening. You probably have so much going on that it is sometimes hard to sort out what you are going to do today let alone in the future. Ask many adults what they want to do in life (realistically!) and you are likely to find similar levels of confusion.

However, like it or not, you do have to think about this kind of thing sometimes, as during Years 10 and 11 you will have to make crucial decisions about what you do next: stay on at school, try to get a job, go to college, or run away and join a circus.

Career wish-list

Translate what you have said about your career ideas into a score using the scale of 0 to 10, with 0 = a total blank in your mind and 10 = you have already signed up to be the next big star in your favourite soap. Keep a record of how your ideas change and develop by filling in the following table at regular intervals.

Date	Career certainty score	Comment – especially on changes

5 What's the big deal about work?

School and work are not the same. It is useful to compare the two. Will you feel very different at work compared to the way you feel at school? Will it be easier or harder? Will you be treated differently? Will you have to act differently?

For a start, at work you may have to dress differently than at school.

Over to you

Jot down some brief notes about a typical day for you at school. Think about the things you do, the way people treat you, and maybe something about your feelings.

Compare your notes with a friend. Do you see things in a similar way?

Find someone in your class who works. Maybe they have a paper round, a part-time job, or do jobs at home. Perhaps they are an active member of a club or society out of school. Give them no more than three minutes to describe what they do and how people treat them when they do this role. They should also consider what they feel about what they do. Jot down in the box below the main things you find out.

Research

Find an older person who has a full-time job in the **public**, **private** or **voluntary sectors**. Get them to describe their feelings on the first day of a new job. How were they treated? Was it easy or hard to fit in? What did they feel like at the end of their first day? Write down the main things you found out in the box below.

Review time

Discuss what you have found out with other members of your group. Knowing about the kind of organisation someone works for usually tells you something about what particular jobs are like and thinking about this might have changed the way that you think about work. If so, you might want to add or change the career wish list you started on page 19.

Public sector: most schools in this country are financed by the government. It is the same with the National Health Service (NHS), police and local government. Any service that is provided in this way is said to be part of the public sector.
Private sector: the private sector consists of all those organizations that are owned by individuals. This can range from large companies like Tesco to the shop on the corner of your road (if you have one!).
Voluntary sector: the voluntary sector (and this is where it gets confusing) consists of organizations which employ both paid and unpaid workers and are usually involved in trying to make people's lives better. Oxfam, Help the Aged and the RSPCA could be described as being part of the voluntary sector, as might your local Girl Guides group or local league football team.

6 Different working environments

In the same way that different businesses do things differently, working environments can also differ. Jobs are often classified according to the stage of production they are associated with. These categories are:

Primary sector – to do with obtaining raw materials (for example, mining, agriculture, and fishing).

Secondary sector – manufacturing (making things).

Tertiary sector – service jobs such as hotels, restaurants, selling – all the processes involved in getting goods and services to the final consumer.

There are obvious differences between jobs in these different sectors. For example, many primary jobs are carried out outdoors. A job in the secondary sector might involve working in a factory or making things on a smaller scale. More importantly, there are overall trends which affect the kinds of jobs that are likely to be available. Manufacturing jobs have declined in recent years whereas service jobs are growing. However, all jobs are different as the following case study shows.

CASE STUDY

There has been a significant growth in jobs in call centres over the last ten years. These might involve **direct selling**, dealing with complaints or other aspects of customer care. Working in a call centre can be quite pressured and workers often have to stick to very strict guidelines including target times for answering and responding to calls. Workers may have to deal with angry and confused customers and will always have to do their best to be both polite and helpful to callers. Good employers recognize the stresses and strains of such jobs and try to ensure that workers are given regular breaks, that their tasks are alternated and good training is given. Some call centre and other service sector jobs are well paid, providing workers with some compensation for doing a tough job.

Over to you

Would you like to work in a call centre? Summarize your thoughts in the box below with reasons for your answer.

Research

Choose two different workplaces and find out what it is like to work in that sector. Describe the working environment of each and say how this might affect what it would feel like to work in each.

Review time

Has this given you any more thoughts on the kind of job you would like? Use the box below to record your thoughts. You might want to reflect on the earlier judgements you made about skills and careers choices on pages 15 and 19.

7 Business objectives

Work experience is likely to be a key element of work-related learning and enterprise education. To get the most out of work experience it is useful to have a basic understanding of how businesses work. Throughout this book the term 'business' is used in the widest possible sense. You can look at your school as a business, while Arsenal can be seen not just as a football team but also as a business enterprise. The same can be applied to the fire service, charities or your local playgroup.

It is important for you to begin to have an understanding of how businesses are organized. This has a big impact on the nature and skills required in different kinds of jobs, and it may affect you choice of career.

Business objectives

All businesses exist for a purpose. When we talk about **business objectives** we are really asking questions such as 'Why does this organization exist?' and 'What do they do?'. Sometimes the answers are obvious. On the other hand it is harder to define the objectives of some organizations.

Research

Use the Internet or any other appropriate sources of information to find out as much as you can about the objectives of a business of your choice. Record what you find out below.

Over to you

Try the following: use pencil first and make a guess at the main objective of the following organizations.

Organization	Main objective
Microsoft	
Tesco	
A local hairdresser	
Your school	
Arsenal Football Club	
Cheltenham General Hospital	
West Thanet District Council	
Greenpeace	

Discuss your responses with a friend. Modify your choices if need be and when you are clear of your answer, confirm your responses in pen.

The right answers

There are no 'right' answers. However, it is likely that the term **profit** has been used, especially in relation to one or all of the first three organizations in the table above. Many organizations have to make a profit in order to survive, and, if you think about it, this will include charities, sports clubs and local government. The other thing that can be said about objectives of organizations is that there is usually more than one. Does Tesco exist just to make as much profit as possible? Why does it help schools to buy computer equipment? Why do schools have budgets? Is making lots of money the only thing that motivates people starting their own businesses?

Knowing the objectives of a particular business is often the key to understanding how and why they do things in particular ways. This has a direct impact in determining what jobs are likely to be available and what working for a particular business might be like.

8 Business organizations

If business studies is one of your subject areas, you might already know something about the functions of businesses. All business textbooks have sections which describe and explain organizational functions. These refer to ways of analysing how businesses are organized by looking at what are often different departments of a business. These usually include:

- finance
- marketing
- production
- administration
- human resources (HR).

The structure of a large business may look something like this.

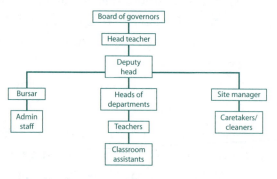

In many ways your school is a business, and the way it is organized reflects this.

Finance

All organizations have to manage and control flows of money. They have to obtain enough money to cover the costs of what they produce or provide. All will have some form of bookkeeping and records of what is spent and earned. Most have employees to pay. This involves calculations about **tax** and **national insurance**. Workers involved in finance sometimes have special qualifications, and it should be obvious they need to be accurate when using figures.

Marketing

This refers to all the processes that are linked to deciding what an organization is going to do and how this is to be communicated to whoever is going to buy or use what is being produced. For example, Apple decided that there would be a big market for MP3 players and invested heavily in producing iPods, which they have convinced many people to buy through memorable television and magazine adverts. Marketing involves predicting what people might buy or need, and includes advertising and promotion.

An Apple iPod.

Production

Production is about making and doing things. All businesses have to work out the best way of making what they produce or providing the service they provide. For example, Ford makes cars in a particular way; Marks & Spencer has recently decided to switch the making of most of its clothes to the Far East; school dinners can be brought in from outside or made on the premises. Production often involves technical expertise such as the skills you might be learning if you do design and technology or engineering.

Administration

Think offices, computers and switchboards – memos, meetings and photocopying. In other words, all the things that have to be done to keep a business running efficiently. People who work in administration are expected to be organized and methodical.

Human resources

Larger businesses usually have specialist departments to look after issues relating to their workers. This might include dealing with the recruitment of new workers, sorting out pay and conditions, as well as setting out what might be done if workers perform badly.

Research

Divide up your group or class and give each person or group the task of finding out more about different organizational functions. In particular, try to identify the different skills required to perform these different functions.

Collect together the results of what you and your group have done and complete the table below.

If you work in:	You will need to be good at:
Finance	
Marketing	
Production	
Administration	
Human resources	

Review time

Has this helped you to decide on the kind of job you would like? Use the box below to record your thoughts. You might want to reflect on the earlier judgements you made about skills and careers choices on pages 15 and 19.

9 Risks and rewards

Risks

One of the main aims of this book is to help you think about yourself and your future. Do you like taking risks?

Over to you

Are you a 'go-getter' or a 'safety first' person?

> I am a real gambler. I love the thrill of not knowing what is going to happen next. If I fail at something, I pick myself up again. School is boring. It is so predictable. I like to keep moving. Sometimes, other people cannot keep up with me.

> I like order in my life: knowing what is going to happen next, keeping on top of things. I have given a lot of thought to my future, even to the extent of thinking about settling down and starting a family.

It is unlikely that you fit into either of these extremes, but you probably lean more to one extreme than the other. Does it matter? Does it affect the kind of job that you might like to do or how you might organize your life? Sum up your attitude to risk below.

My attitude to risk is: _____

_____

because: _____

_____

Rewards

The reward or pay you get from different kinds of jobs is sometimes related to the amount of risk you have to take. There can be a trade-off between risks and potential rewards.

Over to you

You have just been approached by 'Boston Teaparty' to take out a **franchise** to run a coffee shop. You have to put up £50,000 to buy a five-year lease and agree to buy all the things you sell from the franchiser, who will also take 20 per cent of your profits. The potential reward is that the coffee shop could earn you £100,000 a year income.

Discuss in your group whether or not you would invest £50,000 in a franchise like this one. Record your reactions (with reasons) in the box below.

Franchises

These are relatively common business arrangements whereby the franchisee benefits from trading under the brand image but has to deal exclusively with the franchiser. Some branches of the Body Shop are franchises.

Anita Roddick founded the Body Shop, a well-known franchise.

Research

Work as a group and find out as much as you can about the risks and rewards associated with the following jobs:

- a charity fundraiser
- running your own business
- teaching
- working for a building society
- driving a bus.

Do the jobs you investigated carry similar risks and rewards? Summarize your findings in the box below.

10 Size matters

The experience of working for a big organization is very different from working for a small one. In the UK, the biggest employer is the NHS. In fact, the NHS is the largest employer in Europe and the third largest in the world. The NHS provides approximately 1.2 million jobs.

On the other hand, you might know people who own and run their own businesses. These are often called one man or one person businesses. What are the advantages and disadvantages of working for a big or a small organization?

Some businesses consist of many people, and others of only one or two. What could be the advantages and disadvantages of each?

Over to you

What things come to mind? Work in a group and use the table below to pencil in possible advantages and disadvantages of working for big organizations such as the NHS, WH Smith or General Motors (Vauxhall).

Advantages	Disadvantages

Do the same for working for a small business like a hairdresser, village store or body repair shop.

Advantages	Disadvantages

Research

Work with a friend and interview at least two adults – one who works for a large company and one who works for a small company. Find out as much as you can about the pros and cons of working in each and summarize your findings below.

11 Motivation – why even think about working?

What would it be like to live a life of leisure? No work, nothing to do? How real is this? Most people choose to work, but why?

Money is one reason why people work, but scratch beneath the surface and you will find out that attitudes and motivations towards work are more complex. **Motivation** is also a key factor in affecting how effective businesses are. Put very simply, well motivated workers enjoy work and are more productive.

Business studies students might be familiar with the psychologist Abraham Maslow. He wrote about motivation and argued that there are four broad human needs that might be satisfied by work. In other words, there are four main reasons or motivations for people to work.

He arranged these needs in a pyramid, with meeting basic needs at the bottom and a notion of being a happy, contented and fulfilled human being at the top. This is because he argued that some needs are more important than others and so must be addressed first. Once one need is met, we will be motivated to move up the pyramid and meet the next need. He used fancier language but his **hierarchy of needs**, as shown opposite, is a useful way of looking at what work might offer you.

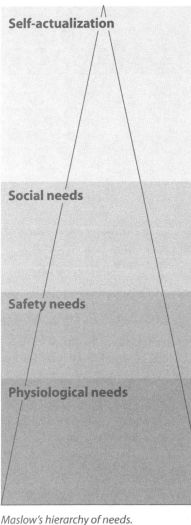

Self-actualization	**Self-actualization:** this is the final need and is only met once all the other needs have already been met. This is the happy, contented person part and refers to getting the job you have always dreamed of or doing something you have always wanted to do.
Social needs	**Social needs:** once physiological and safety needs are met, people are motivated to work in order to fulfil social needs such as friendship, affection and a sense of belonging.
Safety needs	**Safety needs:** this might mean security such as a secure job, savings, health insurance and owning your own home.
Physiological needs	**Physiological needs:** these are the basic needs that must be met before any other need. These might be food, shelter and clothing. So, at the very least, people need to work to pay for these things.

Maslow's hierarchy of needs.

Over to you

What do you think? What motivates you? What do you want to get out of a job? Is it just a means for earning enough money to get by? Do you worry about security? What about needing to belong somewhere? Put Maslow's four needs in order of importance to you.

1 _____

2 _____

3 _____

4 _____

12 Work experience – long-term planning

Almost all school students do work experience, but there are all sorts of different ways in which this is organized. Sometimes work experience happens at the end of Year 10; sometimes at the beginning of Year 11, and some students take a day off normal studies each week for a whole year to learn more about work. For some people, work experience is a life-changing experience.

> I always wanted to work with animals, but then I found out I could not cope with the blood.

> It was brilliant! I was given a real job to do and the atmosphere was so different to school.

> Boring, it did my head in. I wasn't going to bother about my GCSEs, but I am going to stay on now to get the qualifications to get me a better job.

To some extent, what you get out of work experience is a matter of luck, but there are things that you can do to make sure you benefit as much as possible. Ideally, you should choose and organize your work experience, but some schools do it all for their students. Even so, you should plan ahead and think as widely and as imaginatively as possible.

Work experience can help sort out possible career options. Make sure you get all that you can from it. If you have made up your mind on a particular career, it always pays to start thinking about your **CV** and/or **UCAS** application as early as possible.

Over to you

Read and think about the following prompts.

When does work experience take place?

There is no set time for work experience, but many schools take time out at the end of Year 10 or the beginning of Year 11. The point is that it can take a long time for all students to get work placements sorted, and, if you have particular ideas as to what you want to do, you will need to start planning at least six months and up to a year prior to work experience.

How long is it for?

Usually one week but sometimes longer. Some schools plan for two weeks and you may even decide that you want to arrange extra work experience for yourself. A minority of schools do not have a week or two set aside for work experience, preferring to rely on other ways of giving you experience about work, but all students should have some way of finding out more about what the world of work is actually about.

Preparing for work experience

Looking back at all the things you have done so far in the book, and any other ideas you might have about work, where would you most like to do work experience?

Put down three possible choices.

1 _____
2 _____
3 _____

Skills review

Return to pages 15 and 19 to the skills check and career plan to check progress and to help plan what you are going to get out of work experience.

Identify up to three things you want to get out of work experience.

1 _____
2 _____
3 _____

13 Getting the most out of work experience

This section is designed for you to work through a few weeks before work experience is due to start. By this time you should be all prepared, but, if not, there is still time.

Work through these questions to help you get the most out of your work experience. If you have detailed answers to them all, you are well set. If there are gaps, you will have some action points to sort out.

1. Where are you going for work experience?

2. How do you get there?

3. When are you expected?

4. Who do you report to?

5. What will you wear?

6 What do you know about your placement? For example, what do they do? How many people work there?

_____
_____

7 What do you know about what you are going to do?

_____
_____

8 How are you going to cope with nerves before you go?

_____
_____

9 Think about what the company does – what skills will you need?

_____
_____

10 What time do you finish work?

_____
_____

11 How will you get home?

_____
_____

12 Are there any other key issues?

_____
_____

Your work experience will be a valuable and enjoyable experience – you will not be taken for granted!

Doing it

Your school may provide you with a logbook to record what happens during work experience. Use this or the pages that follow to spend ten to fifteen minutes at the end of each day to keep a diary of your experiences. The questions are simple, but this is an exercise you *must* do. There are a number of reasons for this.

- It is good for you to spend some time actually thinking about what you have been doing and your reactions. You might have learned something new about yourself.

- Your subject teachers may want to use your experiences for work in their subjects.

- When you apply for a real job or for university or college, it is a good idea to talk about work experience as it provides evidence of how you coped and learned about the world of work.

1 What did you do on each of your work experience days?

   _____
   _____
   _____
   _____
   _____

2 What did you learn about life at work?

   _____
   _____
   _____
   _____
   _____

3 What did you learn about yourself?

_____

_____

_____

_____

_____

Summary of your work experience

At the end of your work experience, read through your diary. Try to think of five points to describe how it was for you – include positives and negatives (if there were any) but put them in order of importance.

Positives	Negatives
1	1
2	2
3	3
4	4
5	5

Skills review

It would be a good idea to revisit your skills development at this point by going back to Section 2 and filling in the table on page 15.

14 Problem-solving

By now you may well have completed work experience and you should have a clearer idea about employability and enterprise skills. Now is the time to sharpen them up. Let us start with problem-solving.

To recap, you should have learned that:

- being at work is different to being a student
- you are more likely to be interested in certain types of jobs rather than others
- you have greater awareness of your own skills and capabilities
- you should be developing an understanding of enterprise and decision-making
- different kinds of businesses are organized differently.

It is now time to get a better idea of how business organizations might react to different kinds of challenges.

For this activity, your class will be divided up into different groups and you will all be faced with a problem that will require a solution. There is no correct answer, but in undertaking this business challenge you should further develop your skills and understanding of how businesses work.

There will be two different stages to completing this challenge. First you need to find out more about supermarkets and how they compete. Next you need to come up with possible ways (a strategy) for Sainsbury's to regain market share.

The business challenge

Profits collapse at Sainsbury's

Sainsbury's have used Jamie Oliver to advertise their products.

You work for Sainsbury's and some people have judged that the company has been having problems. You have been losing market share to competitors, especially Tesco. Marketing attempts, using celebrities such as Jamie Oliver, to change the image of the company have not reversed falling market share and there is speculation that the company may be subject to a hostile takeover bid.

Profits have not been large enough to invest in a programme of store modernization and there are fears that the main competitor, Tesco, will continue to grow and that other competitors, such as Asda and Morrisons, will also attract Sainsbury's traditional customers. The managing director has called for a major review of the performance of the company and asked a strategy team to suggest a survival strategy.

Stage 1: Get to know your market

Task 1: Research

Work in groups to research Sainsbury's and its major competitors. Within each group, divide different tasks to individuals or pairs.

1 Visiting a local branch of your store.
2 Talking to customers.
3 Searching the Internet.
4 Checking out stories in the financial press.

For each of you, the task is simple – you need to find out why Sainsbury's might be losing market share to its competitors. It is up to you what questions you ask and what information you collect.

Task 2: Putting your ideas together

Staying in your groups, choose a **managing director**, administrator and secretary, and collect together everything you have found out. Your managing director should then prepare a brief report to the whole of the class. You might use PowerPoint, flip charts or a white board to display your evidence. You should start by saying: 'We think that Sainsbury's is losing market share because…'

Stage 2: Developing a strategy

Still working in groups, you need to take on new roles. Each group should take on the role they would associate with the following organizational functions. Within each group, you need to come up with a list of suggestions for improving your area of the business.

- Production
- Marketing
- Finance
- Human resources
- Strategy group.

Production

You will focus on **supply chain** issues and look at how Sainsbury's might source their products. Companies like Sainsbury's rely on other businesses to supply them with goods. Therefore, you are likely to suggest various changes relating to their suppliers and the price customers pay.

Marketing

You should look at why people are shopping elsewhere looking at Sainsbury's image and how and what it tells customers about itself.

Finance

You will focus on profitability. This means how much money Sainsbury's makes. For example, you might want to think about the difference between the prices Sainsbury's buys its goods for and what it sells them for, the cost of actually selling goods and the cost of running the business (staff, utilities, rent and so on).

Human resources

You need to pay attention to the training, **turnover**, customer service, recruitment of staff and wage rates.

Strategy group

You have a different job. First you need to agree on the problems facing Sainsbury's by undertaking a SWOT analysis. Then your main job is to receive reports from the other groups and, from their suggestions, come up with a plan for improving Sainsbury's performance. Present your preferred improvement strategy to the rest of the class. Remember, anything is possible – there are no right answers!

SWOT analysis

This is a common technique used to help the planning process. The 'S' and the 'W' refer to the strengths and weaknesses of a business, and the 'O' and 'T' apply to outside opportunities and threats which might affect a business. The idea is that using a chart like the one below, you list all the strengths and weaknesses of the business, then the opportunities for the business and finally the threats to the business. You then build on strengths and opportunities, and develop strategies to overcome weaknesses and threats.

Strengths	Weaknesses
Opportunities	**T**hreats

Review time

What have you learned about business problems?

_____
_____
_____
_____
_____

What have you learned about yourself? Do you prefer to work on your own or in a team?

_____
_____
_____
_____
_____
_____

15 Doing it for yourself

This activity requires you to work with a group of students from your class to see how good you would be at running your own business.

This is to be tackled in two stages. The first will be like a dummy run and the second could be, with help from your teacher(s) and other adults, the real thing. This could be the most exciting part of *Work-Wise*.

The work that you do in this section might well be spread over a long period of time. The idea is that you use this booklet to keep a record of key decisions and, most importantly, what you have learned.

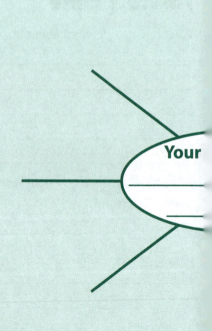

Over to you

Work in a group to produce a **business plan** for running an event to raise money for charity, your school or even yourselves. You could choose from the following list or you could come up with your own idea:

- a concert
- an arts festival
- a sports competition
- a fashion show
- a children's party
- a day at a theme park for your class or a group of younger students.

Choose a fund-raising event to organize.

In your group, decide and agree on the event you want to run. It is up to you how you decide, but at the end of ten minutes you must come up with an idea that everyone in your group agrees with. Produce a spider diagram of your plans, putting your business idea in the centre and including all the different things that you will have to think about.

Research 1

Will your project be viable?

Your group needs to calculate the total costs of running the event. In class, decide on the main things that will have to be paid for. When you have agreed this, fill in the first column of the table below. Delegate tasks for each member of the group and undertake additional research to find out how much things might cost, for example, to hire a hall or to pay for an advertisement.

You may wish to add in an amount of money as a reserve (or contingency) to cover costs you have not thought of. Many businesses set aside 10 per cent of their total budget for contingency costs to cover any unexpected expenses.

Identify each main expense	Estimated amount

When you have all undertaken your agreed research, complete the second column of the table above. Next, estimate how many people you might attract to the event. You should calculate a best and worst case scenario. When you have done this you can decide on your admission charge – or can you?

Research 2
Risk management

Many new businesses fail for a number of reasons, especially because their owners do not identify likely costs. However, if the owners spend time making plans in advance, they can try to anticipate problems or risks. This is called **risk management**.

Spend some time in your group working out whether there is anything that could go wrong when running your event. Think about why the risk might occur and how to take steps to either prevent or minimize any potential harmful effects. Complete the table below, identifying the three greatest risks and possible ways of managing them.

Potential risk	Solution

Use no more than four slides (PowerPoint™ or OHTs) to make a presentation to describe your plans to someone like a local business person or bank manager. In the box below, write down what your group could have done to improve your plan?

16 Business for real

This will be the most effective way of you learning about enterprise and understanding your own strengths and weaknesses in terms of business and employability skills. If you enjoyed the last activity, then this could be even better. You are going to run a business for real.

Getting a business up and running will normally take at least two or three months from start to finish. You could take what you developed in Section 15 and do it for real or you could apply those planning skills to doing something else. You might want to start your own business.

We advise that you complete this activity as a group because this will develop your teambuilding skills and is usually more fun. Each team member should be given a clearly defined role based on the business functions you looked at in Section 8. For example, you will need someone to take responsibility for finance, someone for administration, marketing, production and someone to take overall responsibility for getting things done – a managing director.

Over to you

Get your team together and decide what you plan to do. Before you start arguing about actual products or services, it would be a good idea to 'think outside the box' or do some 'blue sky thinking'. Both these terms refer to trying to think about things differently. Try not to rule anything out and be as creative as possible.

Imagine you have a house brick in front of you. Using a flip chart, a white board or a large piece of paper, brainstorm all the different uses that this could be put to. Remember to record all the possible applications.

The chances are you have generated twenty or more ideas. Now that you have loosened up your minds, do the same thing again but try to come up with a list of at least twenty different ideas for your own business. Remember, do not rule anything in or out. However silly the idea may seem, write it down. Do not spend time thinking about each idea; just write everything down that comes to mind.

Now look over your lists and choose the five best ideas for your business that could be considered in more detail. List these below.

1 _____
_____
2 _____
_____
3 _____
_____
4 _____
_____
5 _____
_____

Research

Get your group members to consider the pros and cons of each of your ideas. Do a SWOT analysis in a table like the one below of each idea to present back to the group.

Strengths	Weaknesses
Opportunities	Threats

Over to you

When you next meet, decide which idea you want to develop further and in the space below list the three most important reasons.

IDEA:

REASONS:

1 _____
_____
_____

2 _____
_____
_____

3 _____
_____
_____

Once you have decided on your business or enterprise activity, you will need to write a **business plan**. This is a document that is designed to help you start your business on the right track by testing whether or not it is likely to be **viable**.

Research

Contact a local bank or look at a high street bank website to get a business start-up pack. This will contain lots of advice on how to produce a business plan. You will need to consider:

- marketing
- production
- start-up costs
- running costs
- possible revenue
- risk management
- pricing.

Get your secretary or administrator to keep a record of all meetings. You do not need to record everything that is said, but it will be helpful to summarize discussions and to clearly identify all 'action points' – that is, who is going to do what and by when.

Running a business will involve disagreements and discussions, and it is important to keep track of what is actually agreed. Also, you will need to record how you overcame problems so you can learn from your mistakes. Again, problems, conflicts and differences are inevitable when you run a business for real.

Three months (or more) later...

After your event, discuss in your group what went well and where improvements could be made. Keep your own record in the box below of what running and organizing an event might have taught you. How did it go? Were you successful? Did you fail? Crucially, what have you learned? Put your thoughts and reflections in the box below.

Skills Review

Go back to page 15 and assess your skills development now that you have completed this activity.

17 Rules in the workplace

Both employers and employees have responsibilities at work and they are expected to follow rules and procedures. If you think about it, all our lives are governed by rules. Some say that if we did not, life would become chaotic. Rules give us structures within which to work. They are meant to help things run smoothly, but inappropriate rules can cause conflict and problems.

Over to you

School rules

Without rules, school life would be chaotic and you would learn nothing.

Working in a group, identify what you consider to be the five most important rules that regulate the way your school works. These can be official (for example, being on time) or unofficial (like Year 11 students sitting in the back seats of the school bus). Record these in the table opposite along with what you believe to be the reason for the particular rule. For example, many schools use bells and buzzers to ensure that the movement between classes is prompt and valuable learning time is not lost.

Rule	Reason

Research

Now think about a particular place of work and try to come up with another list of the five most important rules that regulate the way this business works. Again, these can be official or unofficial rules. State why you think each rule exists and why it might be useful.

Place of work: _____

Rule	Reason

Compare the outcomes from your two lists. Are they similar or different? Are the reasons similar or different? Why do you think this is?

18 Workers' rights

In the same way that our lives are governed by rules, it is also true to say that we have both rights and responsibilities in life. In other words, things that we can expect and things that are expected of us.

Over to you

In the table below, choose three of the most important rights and three of the most important responsibilities you have at school.

Rights	Responsibilities

Discuss in your group whether or not you would like to change any of these. Suggest in the box below how you might go about achieving such a change.

Over to you

There are also rights and responsibilities in the workplace. Some apply to all and some are specific to particular places of work. Before you find out about different rights and responsibilities in an actual workplace, it would be a good idea to have some discussion about your expectations. What rights and responsibilities do you expect to have when you are at work? Agree on the three most important.

Rights	Responsibilities

Lunchbreak, my ass

Press Association
Wednesday 11 May, 2005

Council inspectors are to do spot-checks on Blackpool donkeys to make sure they are getting their full lunch break, officials said today. Councillors discussed what a Blackpool donkey should get for lunch – and decided it should be about an hour. Licensing inspectors will now swoop on the sand to ensure no donkeys are missing out on their employment rights. Council rules state donkeys must only work from 10am to 7pm, have an hour off for lunch, and must get each Friday off. Blackpool Council today denied it was making an ass of itself by upholding the animals' rights and said the rules had been in place for 'donkey's years'.

Research

In a group, find out as much as you can about the rights of employees and the responsibilities of employers in the following areas:

- equal pay
- equal opportunities
- time off for public duties
- maternity and paternity rights
- working hours and holidays
- unfair dismissal
- redundancy.

Use your research findings to produce a leaflet for students in Year 9 entitled 'Workers' Rights'.

On average, women are still paid less than men. Is this inequality of pay fair?

19 Conflict in the workplace

Most people try to avoid conflict. Conflict in the workplace is not in the interest of either employees or employers, and there are many ways by which businesses and workers try to minimize conflict. Sometimes this is hard because of the different interests of those involved. For example, if a worker argues for higher wages, they may be better off but business owners may get smaller profits. Time off for a worker to look after their children is good for the worker and for their children but represents extra costs to the employer.

Strikes or other industrial action may occur if workers feel under-paid or ill-treated. Conflict like this is harmful to both employers and employees and is usually a last resort.

Over to you

Work in a group to identify all the possible causes of conflict at work. You might find it useful to create a spider diagram or mind map to help you. Decide which are the five most serious and suggest possible ways of conflict resolution.

Source of conflict	Possible resolution

Research

Conflict resolution is very different between small and large businesses. Small businesses tend to be more personal and it is usually easier to sort things out before they get out of hand. This is harder to achieve in larger businesses and employers often work with trade unions to establish mechanisms or procedures to deal with conflict. Some of these are also legal requirements (see Section 20). Three examples are given below.

1 Grievance – to be used when a worker feels they have been unfairly treated.

2 Discipline – when the employer considers that a worker is not doing some aspect of their job properly.

3 Accident reporting – systems to be followed as part of health and safety policies to establish fair ways of working out why accidents occur in order to prevent them happening in the future.

Find out as much as you can about one of these procedures in a place of work. Produce a poster or flow diagram to identify the different stages that have to be followed. Discuss the outcomes of your research with other members of your class.

20 Health and safety

All workplaces are governed by rules about health and safety. The law says that all workers have a prime responsibility for their own health and safety and that of other people in the workplace. All workplaces, including schools, are potentially dangerous.

The health and safety executive

Ensuring that workplace environments, such as factories, schools, offices and so on, are safe places for people to work in is the responsibility of the health and safety executive (HSE). They are also responsible for inspecting work premises to make sure that there is no breach of health and safety laws. If they think that unsafe working practices are taking place, they have the power to close down that building/business.

Over to you

Work as a group to undertake a risk assessment of all the potential dangers in the classroom you are in. Choose dangers that might involve three more serious risks and suggest safety measures that could minimize these risks.

Risk	Safety measure

Research

Choose two different workplaces and identify five main health and safety risks that might be associated with each. Then suggest measures to ensure safe working. You might want to choose two very different workplaces like a building site and a small shop; just remember that there are potential risks everywhere.

Risk assessment

A risk assessment is thinking about *what* accidents, dangers or hazards could happen, *when* they could happen, and having steps in place to *prevent* them happening.

Workplace 1

Risk	Safety measures
Example: noise from machinery	*Sound proofing; provide ear protection; provide hearing checks*

Workplace 2

Risk	Safety measures

21 Work can be everywhere!

You can learn about work in all sorts of different contexts including all the subjects that you take.

Vocational and applied subjects like Health and Social Care are very work based – you go on lots of visits, meet health service workers and do assignments that are closely linked to possible jobs. Work is usually less obvious in subjects like maths and history, whereas business, design technology and art might be somewhere in the middle.

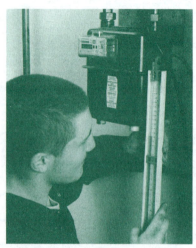

Vocational and applied subjects often offer a 'hands-on' approach to learning.

If you think about it, though, you should be able to identify times when you have learnt about work in all your subject areas. For example, if you take history, did you learn about how fairer working conditions developed over the last century? In maths, your teacher might use budgeting as a means of improving your forecasting skills.

History teaches us how working conditions have changed over time.

Over to you

Complete the table below with examples of work that you have done in other subjects in which teachers use work-related issues to teach their subject. Add your subject areas to the column on the left. Do not worry if you cannot think of anything relating to a particular subject – leave the section blank.

Subject survey

Subject	Example of something linked to the world of work used to help teaching
English	
Maths	
Science	
RE	

Research

Pick two examples from your table on page 63 and summarize what you did in the two tables below and opposite.

Example 1

Subject: _____ **Topic:** _____

Describe what you did:
What did you learn?
Rate how you felt about this lesson (score 0–10 with 0 = the worst and 10 = the best) and comment on whether it made the lesson more interesting or challenging:

Example 2

Subject: _____ **Topic:** _____

Describe what you did:

What did you learn?

Rate how you felt about this lesson (score 0–10 with 0 = the worst and 10 = the best) and comment on whether it made the lesson more interesting or challenging:

Discuss the examples you have given.

Work-related learning should make your lessons more interesting and relevant to your needs. Does it? Record your responses in the box below.

22 Meeting real people

As part of learning about enterprise, your school will probably have arranged a number of opportunities for you to have contact with real business people. For example, schools often organize mock interviews using local employers to give you practice of the real thing. Some schools have special enterprise days involving people from the business community. Trade union representatives and all sorts of other people may be invited into your school.

Each of these opportunities represents a chance to learn more about particular jobs and how businesses work.

Unlike this example, visitors from businesses can provide valuable information about the world of work.

Over to you

Briefly outline what you remember of visits to your school by people from business.

Subject	Visitor – name or title	Business represented	Outline of contribution

Research

Pick *two* of your examples and give more detail of what you actually learned. Make sure these are from two different employment sectors. You might also fill in this section during your visit from a business person.

Visitor: _____ **Business represented:** _____

What did you learn about jobs and working practices?

Does work in this particular kind of business or area of business appeal to you? Explain your answer.

What attitudes, qualifications and skills would you need to be successful in this kind of job?

How was it for you? Give a score between 0–10 (where 0 = the worst and 10 = the best) and explain.

Visitor: _____ **Business represented:** _____

What did you learn about jobs and working practices?

Does work in this particular kind of business or area of business appeal to you? Explain your answer.

What attitudes, qualifications and skills would you need to be successful in this kind of job?

How was it for you? Give a score between 0–10 (where 0 = the worst and 10 = the best) and explain.

23 Same but different

By now you will have been given lots of opportunities to find out that although different businesses have much in common with each other, they also do things in different ways.

Over to you

Work with a group and see how many examples you can come up with to illustrate the idea that different firms might do the same things in different ways. Choose one of the following business practices and compare how two different businesses tackle the same practice:

- recruitment
- promotion
- production.
- dismissal
- selling

How do these methods of production differ?

Business practice: _____

Business 1	Business 2

Research

Think of a business you know something about and investigate how it could improve one of the functions listed opposite. This could be a major piece of research that you might want to link into work experience. You will need to:

- clearly identify the problem
- consider different solutions
- select the best solution
- present your findings.
- explain why it is a problem, for example lost sales

Using a spider diagram may be a useful way of getting an overview of the problem and its impact on the business. Tackling this thoroughly will involve interviews, more research and careful thought. It will also develop your problem-solving skills and generate evidence that can be used to impress at interviews. Students in other schools undertaking this kind of work have come up with imaginative solutions that businesses often do not have the time to consider – so do it!

Summary of problem-solving research

Name of business: _____

Nature of business: _____

The problem and its effects:

Possible solutions:

Preferred solution – why?

24 Should I stay or should I go?

By now you might have some ideas about the kind of job that you would like in the future. So far so good, but what if the kind of job you want is not available, or if pay and prospects are poor? It's time to find out more about the kinds of jobs available to you locally. In other words, you are going to investigate your local **labour market**.

A **market** is a place where buyers and sellers meet to exchange goods. Buyers **demand** goods and sellers **supply** goods. In the labour market, the buyers are employers who want to recruit workers. They create a demand for workers. The sellers are you – the people looking for particular jobs. They supply their services. In some areas of the country demand is greater than supply and in others it is the opposite way round.

In a labour market, the buyers are the employers and the sellers are the people looking for work.

Local unemployment statistics provide key information about the availability of jobs in your area. The big decision is whether you stay in the area in which you live or move away to get the job you want. In other words, is there demand for your services in your area? The best places to start finding out about local jobs are:

- on the Internet – try using a search engine
- your job centre (JobcentrePlus)
- the local newspaper.

Research 1

Using the sources of local labour market information listed above, make a list of the different jobs available for 18 year-olds in your area. Make up a table similar to the one shown below.

Job title	Qualifications required	Pay?	Temporary or permanent?	Further training provided?

What does the information you have collected tell you about the kinds of jobs available in your area? What will prospects be like in the future? Are local industries growing or declining? Are they moving to different areas or even to different countries?

So, do you plan to stay or go? Summarise your findings below

Research 2

You might find it interesting to produce a video or story board to show how jobs have changed in your area over the last 100 years? Are such changes likely to continue in the future?

Use the internet, the library and even your local museum to find out about this. If you study history or business studies, you might already have come across some information that could help get you started.

25 Moving on

In Section 24 you looked at local job opportunities and thought about whether you should stay in your local area or look elsewhere. If you can't do the job you want in the area you live in, you might have to move on. You might go away to work or take up an **apprenticeship**, or you might go to university first and then move away to work. So, it might pay you to consider the pros and cons of leaving your area.

Over to you

Discuss the advantages and disadvantages of leaving your area with other students and identify up to five pros and cons of taking such a decision. Use the table below to give a score to the importance of each point to you, where 0 = absolutely no importance and 5 = something that is top of your priorities

Arguments for leaving (pros)	score	Arguments for staying (cons)	score
Total		Total	

By adding up your scores you can see whether the pros outweigh the cons or whether it is the other way round. Obviously, making such a decision for real would take more time and thought, but the method above is a good starting point.

Research

One of the key factors to consider when deciding whether to 'stay or go' is the demand for particular kinds of workers in different parts of the country in relationship to the supply or number of people who are looking for that kind of work. So, if you want to work in an office, drive a bus or be a teacher in London for example, there are almost always vacancies which employers want to be filled. On the other hand you may find more people wanting jobs in the media in Devon and Cornwall than there are actual vacancies to be filled.

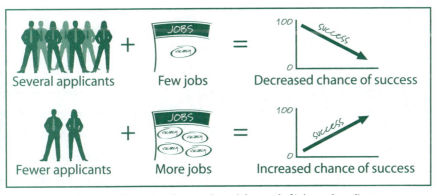

Your chances of success depend on the supply and demand of jobs and applicants.

Choose a possible career path that appeals to you and use the Internet to investigate the availability of jobs in three different parts of the country, including your local area and London. Try typing in 'job vacancies', the job which appeals to you and the area of your choice

Summarise your findings in the box below and end with a judgement on the significance of your research for you.

26 Getting ready for the careers interview

At some point in Year 10 or 11 you are likely to have a guidance interview to help you plan the next steps of your career or education. This section is designed to help you get the most out of this experience.

Over to you

Look back through this guide and think about the progress you have or have not made when it comes to thinking about work and possible careers. You might have done work experience and a range of other activities to help you learn about the world of work. Your views and ambitions might have changed. You should know more about what you are good at, could be good at and what is a lost cause. Similarly, you should be clearer in your own mind about the kind of job you want. Do you want to run your own business, work in a big business, stay at home and so on? Sum up your feelings about possible careers in the box below.

The pie chart below shows what students nationally chose to do after finishing Year 11 in 2004.

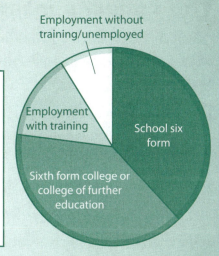

School sixth form = 38%

Sixth form college or college of further education = 39%

Employment with training = 14%

Employment without training/unemployed = 9%

What will be your next step? It is worth giving some thought to the pros and cons of each. Work with a friend and come up with three positives and three negatives about each of these 'progression routes'. When you have done this, use the table below to prioritise your favoured choices, giving reasons for your answers. Think about what your long-term career goals might be and what steps you need to take next to help you achieve them.

Priorities after Year 11	Possible career choice	Reasons

The careers interview

Careers interviews are very useful in helping you to decide which pathway is best for you. Your interview should help in the following ways.

1 Impartial careers guidance – you should not be pushed in a particular direction, but your interviewer should help you to be realistic about suitable careers.

2 The interviewer will have inside knowledge about different career options, college courses and types of higher education courses.

3 The interviewer will also have the skills and experience to encourage you to consider a variety of options.

However, you need to be aware that:

- the interviewer will not be able to sort your life out for you – all they can do is help you to explore options
- they will not necessarily know the answers to everything, but they should be able to find out and let you know.

Research

Think about the advice given above and list what you want to get out of your guidance interview – this should consist of between three and five questions. They might be about qualifications, job prospects, discrimination, pay or further education and training. Use the table opposite to record these and the answers you get from the interview.

Question	Answer

27 Applying for a job

Most employers have standard ways of inviting people to apply for jobs. These can be broken down into two categories.

- Informal applications – where you are asked to phone or even visit the potential workplace. This is more likely to apply to part-time or casual jobs. You will sometimes see posters outside McDonald's and similar places that might say: 'Recruiting now – call in today'.

- Formal applications – employers have to be able to show that they treat applicants fairly and this usually means they will have formal procedures that will be applied when job applications are made. Most commonly, businesses use application forms to decide who they are going to interview.

Whichever approach is used, it will pay you to prepare well.

Informal applications

In spite of what the advert might say, do not rush in – think about it first. First impressions are crucial. You should think about the following points.

- Are you dressed appropriately?
- Do you know what you are going to say when you first go in?
- What questions will they ask?
- What questions will you ask?
- Do you really want to work there?

Even if it only takes five minutes, it is worth sorting out answers to these questions before you rush in.

Formal applications

Most businesses will use more formal means to recruit staff. These usually involve:

- application forms
- letters of application
- **CVs**.

Application forms

This will involve filling in a form to answer questions about the qualifications you have or are working towards, your hobbies and interests, why you want the job and giving your contact details. Once you have returned the form, you may be called in for an interview. There are some commonsense 'dos' and 'don'ts' about filling in application forms.

> Do:
> - give yourself time to do a good job – perhaps fill in the form first using pencil and then fill it in with pen once you are happy with your answers
> - be neat and accurate
> - make sure your spelling and grammar are both good
> - answer all the questions
> - tell the truth, but try to make your answers more interesting than anyone else's.

> Don't:
> - undersell yourself
> - try to be someone you are not
> - be arrogant.

Above all, try to consider what the person reading your application will think about you. For example, if you are applying to work in a chemist, customers might ask you about cures for illnesses and you would need to show somehow that you are responsible and mature. Think about experiences you have had in and out of school that might show this.

You might not think so, but things like babysitting or having a paper round can be used as evidence that you can be mature and responsible.

Over to you

Think of a job. Identify three of the things an employer might be looking for. What have you done that might show you have the skills or attributes required? Complete your answers in the table below.

Job: _____

Desired attribute/skill	Possible evidence

This is a useful exercise to carry out when you are considering applying for jobs.

Letters of application

In many ways, these are harder to complete than application forms. It might help if you use some of the information above as a guide. You should include:

- your full contact details
- which job you are applying for
- why you want the job
- why you are qualified to do it.

Try not to make any mistakes in your letter. When employers receive loads of applications, they have to find ways of cutting down the number of people they want to interview. It is possible that your application will be rejected if it contains mistakes – harsh but true.

This sounds simple but it is not. You would be amazed at the poor quality of letters of application written by adults who should know better!

Over to you

Below is a letter of application. However, there are several deliberate errors or omissions. Find as many as you can and mark each one with a red pen.

> 12 Hornbeam Close
> Evesham
> Worcestershire
> EV
>
> Miss Jan Fryer
> Personal Manager
> Sainsbury
> 17 Fleet Way
> Evesham
> Worstershire
> EV1 5HT
>
> 16th May 2005
>
> Dear Jan
>
> I wish to apply for the post which was advertised in the Evesham Times last Friday.
>
> I am 16 years of age and am in year 11 at Evesham High School. I am taking my GCSEs in June and hope to take business studies at the Technical College next Sept. I am a school prefect and form representative on the school counsel.
>
> I do a paper round with Sykes Newsagents and also baby sit regular.
>
> Yours
>
> Sophie Howes
> x

CVs

Some employers will ask you for a curriculum vitae – usually known as a CV. This is a list of the experiences you have had. It is good practice to provide a covering letter with your CV, like a correct version of the letter of application on page 81. Although there is no one accepted way of producing a CV, the following rules apply.

- It must be neat and accurate.
- Do not lie – you can get caught out.
- You should adapt your CV to fit the skills the job requires.
- It must be easy for the reader to use – at this stage, yours should not be longer than one side of A4.

Similar to the application form and the letter of application, a CV should be adapted to suit the job you are applying for and should include:

- your name
- your date of birth
- your education to date – this would include listing the school you go to, what courses you are taking and what grades you have achieved
- your skills – you should adapt these to fit the job. For example, a job advertisement might say that it requires someone with good interpersonal skills; what experiences have you had in dealing with different kinds of people?
- your hobbies and interests – do not make this up as interviewers often ask about such things at the start of an interview to help you relax.

CURRICULUM VITAE

Sam Jackman

77 High Street
Dartmouth
Devon TQ6 OJY
Home tel: 01803 516032
Mobile: 07719 913770

Relevant experience

2003–05
(On several occasions)   Voluntarily worked for local MP in busy office. Jobs included answering telephone, replying to letters and organizing files.

June 2004   Worked at Mary Rose's Pottery Plant for one week of work experience. I tried many different things – making pottery, cleaning up, serving customers and pricing work in the gallery.

I have also helped my father with his business on many occasions, answering the telephone, making phone calls and filing documents.

Education

2001–05   I attend Chew Magna School in Dartmouth and will take ten GCSEs in June 2005. I have predicted grades of Bs for English, Maths, Science, History, Art and Textiles, Technology, and a C in German.

Achievements   I was awarded a certificate at school after work experience for obtaining several skills, including excellent attendance, punctuality and safety awareness.

Interests   I have many interests, particularly in fashion. I also like shopping, reading, travelling and regularly swim at my local pool.

References

Lucy Duffy	Ms Williams
MP's Office	Head of Yr11
Belle Vue Centre	Chew Magna School
Torbay	Dartmouth
Devon	Devon

A curriculum vitae (CV).

Over to you

Prepare your word-processed CV and keep an electronic version for future use. You can use the CV above as a guideline.

28 Interview technique

Going for your first interview (in fact, any interview!) is scary. You are putting yourself on the line. You might really, really want the job or the place on the course. So you have to be prepared for the unexpected.

It might help if you consider interviews from the point of view of the person who is going to interview you. What do they want to get out of the interview?

An employer's perspective

From a business point of view, the problem is quite simple. Interviews cost time and money. The law requires me to treat applicants fairly and equally. I am also a busy person and I want to find the most appropriate person for the job who isn't going to go off travelling in a month's time. When it comes to the interview, I want to see the real person, so my first job is to try to put them at ease – you can't interview someone who is a bundle of nerves.

It is important to keep the last bit of the quote in your mind. It is very unusual for an interviewer to set out to catch you out or show you up, as this would make you even more nervous. They will actually give you opportunities to show why you are the person for the job. You can expect them to start with a general question about school life or something you are interested in.

The other thing that needs to be said over and over again is that work and school are different. In school you are often judged as being the best or worst at something, but when it comes to an interview you might not be the best or the worst but you will be the person the interviewer is looking for. There is a difference! You could be rejected because the employer thinks you are too clever or too ambitious.

So, where does this leave you? Prepare thoroughly and give it your best shot.

Things to do

- Know as much about the job beforehand as possible – read the job specification and any information carefully, and list the five main things they appear to be looking for. Think of things you have done that show you have these kinds of skills and attributes. For example, if you are expected to work on your own, what examples would you give to show that you can do things for yourself?

- Listen to the questions and try to give an appropriate answer. Think back to your list of what you have done and your skills and attributes.

- Think positively! Say to yourself that you are the right person for the job. If you get asked a difficult question, be upfront and ask them to explain it. Say, 'I need to think about that…' or 'Do you mean x, y or z?'

- Dress right. Find out about the dress code for the employer and dress accordingly. You should look smart and business-like.

- Prepare a couple of questions – about pay, prospects, holidays, training … anything like that – and do not be afraid to ask them.

- Watch your body language. Shake hands, wait to be told to be seated, bring your legs together, keep eye contact with the interviewer, do not fiddle or twitch and try not to slouch.
- Be polite and interested.
- Last but not least, breathe, smile and try to relax!

Interviewers are not there to try and catch you out – they want you to show what you have to offer.

Over to you

Discuss these suggestions in your group. Do you agree with the advice? Note below the three most important things for you and explain your reasons. Did you think of any other things to do in an interview? If you did, list them.

Research

Using some real job details and an application form, work out how you would prepare for an interview. You might get these from your teacher or by requesting an application form for an advertised position. Think about knowing about the job, what you would wear and questions you might ask. Record your answers below.

Interview for: _____

Advice	
Preparation	
Clothes	
Questions	

29 Perils of plastic

Many young people use plastic, debit and credit cards as the main means of paying their way. Some young people have debts. Unplanned debts can be horrendously expensive but with some planning these can be avoided.

Paying for things

Debit cards

If you use a **debit card** the amount you spend is immediately taken from your bank account. Sometimes it is hard to keep track of what you have spent and it is easy to go into overdraft. You can also withdraw cash with a debit card.

Overdraft

An **overdraft** is when you owe money to a bank because you have spent more than you have in your bank account. You have to pay interest on an overdraft and rates vary widely. On an authorised overdraft, which is agreed with the bank, you might be charged around 10 per cent interest per year. This means you will pay an extra 10 percent of what you owe. On unauthorised overdrafts you might pay a higher interest rate and will also be charged a fine for every time you go further overdrawn. For example, if your overdraft limit is £100 and you have gone up to £110 overdrawn, you might be charged a £20 fine and a further £20 every time you go further overdrawn.

Credit card

A **credit card** allows you to pay for things in a similar way to a debit card. You can pay in person, over the phone or on the internet. However, a credit card allows you to buy goods without paying for them immediately. The credit card company will pay for the goods, then you pay them later. You get a monthly bill and if you pay this off right away you don't get charged interest. If you don't pay the full amount on the bill, you will be charged interest on what you owe. You can pay anywhere between 8 and 30 per cent interest for money borrowed on a credit card. Here is an example: you owe your credit card company £100. You can't pay it off when the bill comes and the credit card company charges around 25 per cent interest on an annual basis. So, you now owe the company £100 + £25. This would mean that you would be charged around £3 a month extra until the balance is paid off. You may also have to pay a fee if you miss a payment.

CASE STUDY

Kim has a degree and has just started his first job as a trainee journalist. He takes home £800 a month. He has a credit card and owes £1100. The minimum monthly payment is £30. He still has an overdraft from the time that he was at university.

Kim got a letter yesterday from his bank saying that he had exceeded his £1500 overdraft and would have to pay £20 a day as an unauthorised overdraft fee.

Kim gets his first pay cheque in two weeks time.

Over to you

What can Kim do? Who is at fault? How could this situation be avoided?

(1) Imagine you are in a similar position to Kim and complete the simple budget below. You will need to work out how much you would spend on these different parts of your budget. It might be fun to do this as a spread sheet, as you can then show the impact of changes in Kim's finances. Don't forget about the interest rates and bank charges.

	September	October	November	December
Opening bank balance	– £1550			
Wages	800	800		
Other income				
Total income	800			
Living expenses				
Housing				
Utilities				
Food				
Transport				
Mobile phone				
Clothes				
Bank charges				
Credit card				
Emergencies				
Total expenses				
Monthly cash flow (total income – total expenses)				
Balance at end of month (opening balance + monthly cash flow)				

(2) Work as a team and produce a leaflet for those leaving school titled 'How to avoid debt'.

30 Conclusion

You might think that it is all over: exams coming up; next steps planned. You might even be thinking about a holiday! However, there are two ways of looking at where you are now. You are at both an end and a beginning. If things have gone well your next moves should be clearer. Hopefully you will have:

- a clearer idea of what you might want to do as a career
- a better understanding of what you will need to do to reach these goals
- developed skills required in the workplace and in managing your finances
- learned more about the world of business
- gained greater confidence in knowing what you are good at and what you can improve on.

Unfinished business

Making progress in sorting out what you want to do also brings new challenges. You may have concerns about:

- getting the grades you need
- starting afresh in the sixth form, at college or at work
- meeting new friends.

Even though you might be staying on at your school, others will be leaving and in lots of ways the end of Year 11 will be a turning point in your life. What are your feelings about the future? Jot down your thoughts in the box on page 92. You might also look at the list at the top of the page to give you some prompts.

Finally

Think about keeping hold of *Work-Wise*. You may find it useful when applying for jobs or preparing for interviews. And last but not least – good luck!

Glossary

apprentice a person learning a skilled practical trade from an employer

attributes general qualities and characteristics that help to make us the person we are

benchmarking measuring progress or performance against an established standard

business objectives the reason why a business exists, what it aims for and wants to achieve

business plan a document that summarizes the financial objectives of a business and gives a detailed plan of how those objectives will be achieved

credit card a card which allows you to buy goods without paying for them immediately

CV (curriculum vitae) a list of the experiences and qualifications you have; this document is usually used with a letter of application when applying for jobs

debit card similar to a credit card except money is immediately taken from your bank account

demand the amount of a given product that people would buy

direct selling method of selling that only involves the manufacturer and the customer (no 'middle man')

franchise an agreement by one business to allow another business to sell its products or services

hierarchy of needs a model of motivation developed by Abraham Maslow, showing how people have different levels of needs to motivate them

job description a document setting out the responsibilities of a particular job

labour market the kinds of jobs available

lean business modern term used to describe an efficient business employing as few people as possible

managing director the title usually given to the boss or person with overall responsibility for the day-to-day running of a business

market a place where buyers and sellers meet to exchange goods

motivation the desires and drives that make us want to do things

national insurance compulsory payments made to the government to pay for state benefits such as the NHS

overdraft when you owe money to a bank because you have spent more than the money you put into your bank account; there can be authorised and unauthorised overdrafts

person specification the required and desired skills and experience for a particular job

primary sector the sector concerned with extracting and obtaining raw material such as coal, fish and so on

private sector the private sector consists of all those organizations that are owned by individuals

profit the difference between the total costs of production and the revenue earned from selling products and services

public sector any service or product that is provided by central or local government is said to be part of the public sector

risk management trying to anticipate possible problems or risks to a business and working to minimise them

secondary sector the manufacturing sector, where products are made

supply the quantity made of a given product

supply chain the chain of processes involved in the production and distribution of a product

SWOT analysis a technique where the strengths and weaknesses of a business are listed, and the opportunities and threats to the business are identified

tax money taken by the government to pay for education, roads, the armed forces and so on – for example, income tax

tertiary sector the sector consisting of services

turnover the money raised from the sale of goods or services

UCAS the Universities and Colleges Admissions Service

viable a business idea or plan which is likely to be profitable

voluntary sector sector consisting of organizations which employ both paid and unpaid workers, and is usually involved in trying to make people's lives better

Index

A
accident reporting 59
administration 27
applications for jobs
    application forms 79–80
    CVs (curriculum vitae) 82–3
    formal 78, 79–83
    informal 78
    interview technique 84–7
    letters of application 80–1
apprenticeship 72
attributes 16–17

B
benchmarking 14–15
'blue sky thinking' 51
brain-storming 51
budget 90
business objectives 24–5
business people contacts 66–7
business plan 47, 52
business practice differences 68
'business' - wide use of word 24

C
call centres 22-3
careers
    possible 18–19
    wish-list 19
careers interview 74–7
characteristics 16–17
communication skills 10
conclusion 91–2
conflict at work 58–9
creativity 12, 51
credit cards 88–90
CVs (curriculum vitae) 82–3

D
debit cards 88
debts 88–90
demand and supply 70
direct selling 22–3
discipline 59
donkeys' lunch break 57

E
employability 12
employers
    large 32–3
    small 32–3
ethics 13

F
finance
    budget 90
    credit cards 88–90
    debts 88–90
    organizations 27
    strategy 44
franchises 31
future planning 18–19

G
glossary 93–4
'go-getter' 30
grievances 59

H
health and safety 59, 60–1
hierarchy of needs 34–5
human resources
    organizations 28
    strategy 45

I
ICT skills 10
interviews
    career interview 74–7
    employer's perspective 84–5
    preparation 85–6
    technique 84–7

J
job descriptions 16
jobs
    applications 78–83
    availability elsewhere 73
    away from home area 72–3
    call centres 22–3
    direct selling 22–3
    locally 70–1
    primary sector 22–3
    secondary sector 22–3
    tertiary sector 22–3

L
labour market 70
letters of application 80–1
local jobs 70–1

M
managing yourself 12
market research 43
marketing
    organizations 27
    strategy 44
Maslow, Abraham 34–5
mind map 8–9, 69
morals 13
motivation 34–5

N
national insurance 27
needs, hierarchy of 34–5
numeracy skills 11

O
objectives in business 24–5
one man businesses 32–3
organizing yourself 12
organizations
    large business 26
    school 26
'outside the box thinking' 51
overdraft 88
own business
    practical 50–3
    theoretical 46–9

P
person specifications 16
physiological needs 35
primary sector jobs 22–3
private sector work 21
problem-solving
    overview 42–5
    research 69
    Sainsbury's case study 43–5
    skills 11
procedures 54–5
production
    organizations 27
    strategy 44
profit 25
project viability 48, 52
public sector work 21

R
responsibilities 56–7
rewards 31
rights 56–7
risk assessment 61
risk management 49
risks 30–1
rules 54–5

S
'safety first' 30
safety needs 35
Sainsbury's case study 43–5
school
    business people contacts 66–7
    not same as work 20–1
    organization 26
    rules 54
    work-based subjects 62–5
secondary sector jobs 22–3
self-actualization 35
self-assessment 14–15
self-confidence 14–15
social needs 35
spider diagram 8–9, 69
start-up pack 53
strategy development 44–5
strategy group 45
supply and demand 70
SWOT analysis 45

T
tax 27
team work skills 11
teambuilding skills 50
tertiary sector jobs 22–3
time line 7
timetable 6

U
understanding business 12

V
voluntary sector work 21

W
work
    environments 22–3
    not same as school 20–1
    private sector 21
    public sector 21
    voluntary sector 21
work experience
    benefit from 38–41
    key element 24-5
    planning 36–7
    summary 40–1
work related issues 62–5